"Heart Works" Mindful Things from the Heart

Tonia L. Slaton

Written By: Tonia L. Slaton

© 2017 by Tonia Williams

ALL RIGHTS RESERVED. No part of this book may be reproduced in any written, electronic, recording, or photocopying without written permission of the publisher or author. The exception would be in the case of brief quotations embodied in the critical articles or reviews and pages where permission is specifically granted by the publisher or author.

Publishing Service By: Pen Legacy®

Typesetting By: Junnita Jackson

Cover Design By: Christian Cuan

Library of Congress Cataloging – in- Publication Data has been applied for.

Paperback ISBN: 978-1-7362575-9-3

PRINTED IN THE UNITED STATES OF AMERICA.

Dedication

This book is dedicated to my head and my heart.
I could not be open to love without them both.
God has always been good to me and I thank Him for
this gift.

PREFACE

I begin writing poems in high school. Words would come to me and I would grab a pen and put it to anything that I could get my hands on to write on. But nothing ever became of it.

I would often have words in my head and in my heart but that is where they remained until 2009 when I decided to begin writing again. As I did in high school, I kept a pen handy and would immediately put my words down on any type of paper I could find.

The purpose of this book is to share with readers words from my heart to stimulate the mind of what the heart goes through.

This collection of poems has been in the works since 2009. Between then and now, I have moved to different places, had different jobs, had loss of family and friends and new relationships. Life happened.

I finally decided that it was time for me to share my "Heart Works" and allow readers to experience mindful things from the heart through my words.

In the current world that we live in, I encourage all to stay prayed up, be guardians of your heart, keep an open mind, positive attitude, and allow love to come in.

ACKNOWLEDGEMENTS

I would like to take this opportunity to acknowledge my husband, Dennis Slaton. I shared my poems with him and he encouraged me and prayed for me to get this book published. He is such a blessing in my life.

Special acknowledgement goes to Karmika Triplett who has been instrumental and part of my motivation to start writing again.

I would be remiss if I did not acknowledge two of the most influential people in my life. My son, Deonte Kenneybrew and my daughter, Brianna Roberson. From day one, they have influenced me to be a great mom. I have drawn inspiration from them and the way that they have lived their lives as adults. I have always encouraged them to do their very best and now I am practicing what I preached to them by doing my very best with this book.

Ms. Hattie Williams, without you and the grace of God, there would be no me.

"We do not get to choose whether we make a difference or not because we do.
We do get to choose whether that difference is positive or negative."

~ Author Unknown~

"The Whisper"

Today the wind blew softly
I heard it whisper your name in my ear.
I simply smiled.

You are Loved

Man of honor, standing tall
A loving heart that loves us all.
You carry a proud and noble name
And you deserve to be loved the same.
Regardless of how the world looks around you,
Know that you are loved.

A Soul On Fire

I listened to you talk
And I heard your soul crying.
I saw the tears roll down your face
While all along trying,
Trying to understand your pain.

Listening to your story
My eyes produced a tear.
I dare not allow it to fall,
I just want you to know I am here.

Your soul is on fire
And it hurts me to see
While your soul is on fire,
There cannot be a you and me.

You and I As One

I stare out of the window
And the sky is so clear.
I saw you passing by
And I held by breath.

As I lost sight of you
I slowly began to breathe again.
At that moment, I knew
You and I were one.

"Our First Kiss"

It was soft…..
It was slow…..
It was deliberate…..
It was sensual…..
It was passionate…..
It was deep…..
It was desired…..
It was ours.

Thank You!

Thank you for your honesty!
Thank you for your smile!
Thank you for your tears!
Thank you for your sharing!
Thank you for your heart!
Thank you for your wisdom!
Thank you for loving me!
Thank you for your words!
Thank you for being you!

"Something Between Us"

There is something between us
We both know it to be true,
There is something between us
Between me and you.

There is something between us
It's so clear and plain to see,
This something between us
Right now cannot be.

There is something between us
And it's so hard to say,
We can't share this something between us
At least not today.

There is something between us
And if it's God's will, we will see,
That this something between us
Will one day equal you and me?

"I Am Not Here To Judge"

There is this man
I was chosen to hear his story.
His shoes will never fit my feet.
I don't see him with eyes of judgment,
I see him with eyes of love.

"Nothing To Hide"

I have nothing to hide.
It is as plain as the noise on my face.
I have nothing to hide
And I will say it with grace.
I want what we have between you and me.
I have nothing to hide,
Therefore, I give you complete honesty.

"He Saw Me Coming"

I walked to the bus stop minding
my own business and he saw me coming.
I see him with his eyes all aglow
Because he saw me coming.

Look at him with his nostrils all
Wide, taking in my scent.
He liked it....

He sat next to me on the train trying
To see if our energies were in sync...
They were.

He smiled as he got off of the train
Hoping tomorrow that he would see me coming.

"A Difficult Choice to Make"

She is his little princess, this I know
He had a difficult time choosing whether
To stay or to go,

With this difficult choice to make
It didn't seem right,
And it caused him to wonder
All through the night.

He has a queen that he loves
With all his heart,
But the timing wasn't right
And it kept them apart.

He had a difficult choice to make
And it rocked his world,
But the choice wasn't difficult at all
Because his princess was his little girl.

His Queen understood.

"Doing the Right Thing"

You don't have to feel bad about
Doing the right thing.
Some things in life make us sad
But it's alright.
Some things in life make us mad
But it's alright.
When you are doing the right thing,
Life works out.
Staying prayed up leaves little
Room for doubt.
God will see you through when you are
Doing the right thing.

Letting Go!

My heart is too fragile to break again,
I have to let go, it's the end.
The end of a love that could not be,
The end of the road for you and me.

My heart cannot take another heart break.
I have to let go before the pieces are hard to find.

Letting go…..goodbye.

"Starting Over"

The sky is blue…..
Does this signify happiness?

The sky is grey…..
Is happiness fading?

It is storming outside…..
Is it time to let go?

Letting go of damages, baggage, old stuff,
Dreams deferred…..

Starting the day after tomorrow, all
Things not needed will be let go.

It's time for letting go…..new beginnings
My new life starts immediately.

"The Heart Doesn't Lie"

Unhappiness is not a good feeling.

He is gone, I am miserable, and
    My heart is not healing.

Why does it have to be this way?

Why couldn't we be together?
    Why couldn't he stay?

The heart doesn't lie, I miss him so.

"Things Happen"

He showed up and became apart
Of our lives.
He stayed for a long time.
One day he was gone, never to return.
Things happen…..we moved on.

"He's Here Now"

The only being left that I trust
With my heart is God.
My heart is too fragile to break again.

God knows my heart and that it's weak,
And I have waited patiently for
The blessings that I seek.

And he's here now.

A love that God has brought to me,
He has blessed me so graciously.

He's here now with happiness abound,
To always be around.

I am happy because he's here now.

"Silence and Me"

Silence,
I hear it all around me

Silence,
I must embrace it to find me again

Silence,
It's very loud but no one hears it except me

Silence,
It's me and I hear you.

"Eyes Wide Open"

Today I embraced my loneliness
It wasn't difficult to do.

I must take time to heal because
My wounds are still fresh.

With eyes wide open, I can still
See a future deserving of me.

I see trust, honesty, love, and loyalty.

I will keep my eyes wide open
For when my future arrives.

"I Am Enough"

Situations in life will have you thinking,
Am I enough?

Life experiences, lessons learned.

God made me in His own image
So whatever the situation,
I am enough.

Always have been, always will be.

"His Eyes"

His eyes they see me
With a light of love

A kind of love that shines
From above

His eyes say things that
Cannot be denied

His eyes show things that
He cannot hide

His eyes are windows to
His soul

His eyes show a love so
Very bold

His eyes see me in a
Very special way

His eyes look upon me with
A yearning for a new day

I love it when he looks at
Me with "His Eyes"

"Photographic Memory"

He was scared, curious, and nervous with anticipation.
He was gentle, kind, loving and understanding.
He loved me until the end or perhaps, forever.
What we had is forever etched in my photographic memory.

"All Alone"

Many years passed by,
Happy times were plentiful
One day I looked in the mirror and realized,
I am all alone now.

It was my choice to end it.
If it were up to him, we would still be.
The decision was not easy,
Still, I am all alone now.

And it hurts!

"Exceptional Memories"

The birds are signing,
I am without a single song to sing.
Why are the birds so happy?
While my tears continue to flow.
It is because I have exceptional memories
Of what he and I shared.

The exceptional memories of what we had
Has put a song in my heart.
I began to smile and now,
I am singing like the birds.

"All That I Have"

He promised me something different
It made my heart skip a beat.
All that I am and all that I have
Were words that knocked me off my feet.

He called me his queen
And would have given me the world if he could.
All the I am and all that I have
Was clearly understood.

Years later, it ended.
Now, all that I have……. is me.

About the Author

Tonia Slaton is an avid reader and love to nestle up with a good book while listening to jazz. Her favorite sound is the rain. The rain is a wonderful sound that invites comfort to the ears and mind for writing and putting words to paper. When she is not working, she spends quality time with her family and keeps pen and paper handy just in case thoughts come to mind that need to be in print.

www.ingramcontent.com/pod-product-compliance
Lightning Source LLC
Chambersburg PA
CBHW062207100526
44589CB00014B/2002